Copyright © 2023

DIDAINK

All rights reserved.

ISBN: 9798399767215

Edited with Stacy Pershall

Introduction by:

Dida Gazoli & edited by Nancy LaFever

Cover Art:
acrylic on canvas,
painted by Carrie Barcomb

~ In memory of Don Terner ~

Volume 3

CONTENTS

Editor's Note

by Dida Gazoli

Volume 3 is centered around how men and/or boys influenced the writers as women, daughters, sisters, and mothers. In a world where female voices are often dominated by male declarations, each featured writer had the opportunity to consider how one or more male figures changed them for the better, and sometimes for the worse. Whether they were fathers, sons, employers, pastors, priests, mentors, or even strangers, the common thread sewn into Volume 3 is: we are the individuals we are because of the men or boys who shaped our inner lives, our homes, and our communities.

I used the pronoun "we" because included in this volume is an essay I began several years ago, yet only now had the courage to share. Fear has often stopped me in my tracks, made me turn around and go the opposite direction. Fear is powerful, and it can force you to pretend you don't see the truth in what's ahead: *more anger, regret, and pain*. But truth is also freedom, and freedom is the best chance we have at autonomy in our lives.

Thank you for reading our work and supporting it. May you find consolation here in our true stories, and inspiration too. Veracity, as each of us knows, isn't easy, but it continues to empower change and healing.

Introduction

UNRAVELING THE TRUTH

Dida Gazoli

Mama lifted the heavy meat tenderizer, her fingernails the color of red candy apples, and I worried the hammering would ruin her manicure. She pounded the tenderizer against the wood cutting board like she was wielding an axe and smiled at me. She was somehow relaxed, in control, and powerful like a lumberjack. I knew about lumberjacks like Paul Bunyan and Babe, his trusted blue ox, from the cartoons I watched while Mama got ready in the mornings. I imagined her dressed in blue jeans, a checkered flannel shirt, brown work boots, things she never owned. She was teaching me how to make Sicilian braciole in a cabin hidden deep in the woods. *Daddy would never find us there*, I thought.

She pronounced it "brah-joh-lee," and I remembered her first making them for Christmas and New Year's when my sisters were home from college. She'd learned the recipe from her Italian mother or grandmother, and on those days, Mama

UNRAVELING THE TRUTH

Dida Gazoli

made the kitchen smell like an Italian cucina; a warm, loving place to be. I could almost forget my brothers' screams when she cooked, their bodies slamming against the linoleum, their pain rising through the floorboards and pouring into my little body shaking behind the locked bedroom door.

Mama was the most beautiful woman I'd ever seen. She outlined her full lips with a skinny pink crayon, then colored them in with a bigger red crayon that slept in a shiny gold case. This careful task transformed her mouth into the color of plump cherries. She wore her dark hair in a short, elegant style that accentuated her wide chestnut eyes and smooth olive skin. She'd learned that sophisticated look from the Spanish hairdresser she met the year we lived in Europe. My father was on a paid sabbatical in 1970, and he'd rented us an apartment near Barcelona, Spain. I turned six there and soon realized that Daddy wore two faces: the one with the big white teeth, happy and laughing, and the dark,

UNRAVELING THE TRUTH

Dida Gazoli

purplish-red face that spewed "mortal sins," according to the Third Commandment of my parent's Catholic doctrine.

I also learned Daddy didn't like children who made noise, especially when he was driving. One day I laughed too loud at something my brothers said in the VW van and my father took hold of my face and squeezed so hard it felt like he'd slashed it with a knife. The burning pain left a welt on my face and deep inside my body. *If Daddy loves me, why does he hurt me?*

In Spain, and everywhere else, I felt the safest by my mother's side. My father seemed to adore her like I did—it was the only thing we had in common— and he treated her to nights out on the town to show her off. I loved watching Mama get dressed up, wondering which pair of long earrings she'd choose. I studied how she used the black crayon to make her eyes and long black lashes look a movie star. When she was all done and ready to go, my father would

UNRAVELING THE TRUTH

Dida Gazoli

brag, "Look how beautiful she is," as if he had something to do with it. People often compared her to the Italian actress Sophia Loren, and I wanted Mama to be a real movie star, and rich, so she could take us far away from my father. *Then we'd be safe,* I thought.

On the coveted braciole days, I stood beside her in the kitchen and watched as she turned the cheap cuts of beef my father bought at the Army base into delicious mini roasts. She filled each thin square of beef with minced garlic, parsley, homemade breadcrumbs, and Parmesan cheese. All rolled up in neat rows, the braciole looked like little brown packages waiting to be mailed at the post office. I wanted to slip notes inside each one. *Help us,* they would've said.

I couldn't understand why she stayed with a man so full of anger and capable of such violence. *You're movie-star beautiful, Mama. You could have any man you want. Why can't you leave him?* But during

UNRAVELING THE TRUTH

Dida Gazoli

those days, I never blamed her; I loved her too much. So, I blamed the Catholic church. I hated going to Sunday mass and pretending like we were a wholesome, happy family as we followed my parents into church like ducklings. I'd finally graduated from the soundproof "crying room" and could sit next to my mother in the pew, always on her left side when my father was with us. Sitting in Mama's beautiful shadow made it easier to forget the abuse.

In the 1970s, women couldn't get divorced and still be considered "good" Catholics; they could only hope for an annulment, but that meant my mother would have to petition the church. She'd have to reveal how many children she had and how many years the abuse went on (eight children, 22 years). Telling that truth might also make her responsible in the church's eyes. She'd be judged and her decisions examined under a magnifying glass, because she stayed, year after year, with an abusive man. Petitioning the Roman Catholic church, admitting

UNRAVELING THE TRUTH

Dida Gazoli

the truth, would be an *unraveling*. Unfortunately, my mother cared too much about appearances to risk the "look how beautiful" image. But what if her appearance gave her power over my father? What if it helped calm or influence him in moments I never knew about? In a way, Mama *was* an actress like Sophia Loren. Acting like we were a big, happy family may have been the only way she could cope.

According to my oldest sister, who's 16 years older, my father was consistently warm and loving in the first nine years of her life, though, I knew him as Dr. Jekyll and Mr. Hyde. My sister described how my father was *more* affectionate than my mother with her, but something changed when my sister turned nine. It was the same year my father accepted a job in a new town, and they moved into a new house in 1958. That was the house I was raised in. She was an avid *Nancy Drew* reader, like many girls in the 1950s, and my parents told her that a famous mystery writer, Earl Stanley Gardner who authored *Perry*

Introduction

UNRAVELING THE TRUTH

Dida Gazoli

Mason, owned the house before they moved in. So, my sister blamed her daddy's new, violent behavior on it. *Maybe the house was haunted.*

I, on the other hand, not only blamed the Catholic church, I blamed my mother's family too, especially my grandfather. I never met him, although I was ten when he died. He'd turned his back on my mother in the 1960s, eventually shunning her completely in the years following my grandmother's death. My father was an academic, and an officer in the U.S. military; he knew nothing about farming or fruit ranching, my grandparent's family business. My mother followed my father's teaching career and moved away from her family's ranch. But I remember one particular night – something was about to change.

I was four or five and sitting on the dark stairway beside one of my sisters. There were some blue suitcases at the bottom of the stairs, near the front door. We stayed silent, listening to my parents in the living room, but they couldn't see us. They weren't

UNRAVELING THE TRUTH

Dida Gazoli

shouting, but someone was crying—I can't remember if it was Mama or Daddy—but I had the distinct feeling we were going somewhere, and Daddy wasn't coming with us. Then the blue suitcases went back into the closet.

I realize now that my mother probably didn't have anywhere to go. After her mother died, her father and sister closed the door on her, and there were likely no domestic abuse shelters in the '60s and '70s in our town. If she went to her Catholic parish, it would be too risky; the whole town might find out, putting my father's teaching career in the community at risk. She didn't have enough money to take care of herself, let alone six children under the age of 16. My father's name was on everything; he controlled their finances like most men in those days. Her name may not have even been on the deed to the house. By 1975, when I was 10, she was an occasional substitute teacher, but my father was a tenured college professor. So where would she go?

Introduction

UNRAVELING THE TRUTH

Dida Gazoli

A hotel? For how long? Another house? How would she pay for it? Even though there were credit cards as early as 1950, two years after my parents married, she never had one. My father didn't believe in them. He gave her a cash allowance for groceries, or she would write a check at the store, but she didn't know how to balance a checkbook. He took care of that.

Although I never saw my father physically hit my mother, I learned from two older siblings that she tried to place herself between my father and the child he was beating. She was knocked around in the process. But my father got savvier over the years, and he would hit us when my mother was out shopping or doing errands. No one ever told her what he'd done while she was gone. We too were steeped in fear.

I can't speak for my siblings, but I felt paralyzed inside that house. I dreamt of telling on my father and a new life away from him, but I also felt that if I exposed him, it would make him even angrier, which

UNRAVELING THE TRUTH

Dida Gazoli

terrified me. Like my mother, I developed acting skills to hide the truth from friends and the few family members we had on my father's side. Remaining silent or lying about the abuse calmed my fears and I could function, focus on school, and have a social life. Then, as I became a teenager, I felt safer away from my mother's side. I rode my bike everywhere and walked the streets of our town feeling more confident than I ever did inside our house.

"Where were you?!" My father screamed one night, as I walked through the side entrance and into the kitchen. I was almost 16 then, the last kid still under his roof, and I recognized the steam fulminating from his nostrils. He'd morphed into the bull again, and was charging me. "You goddamn good-for-nothing! Where the hell have you been?" His 6' body towered over my 5'4 frame. My mother was standing right there, but she couldn't get in front of him and over to me in time.

Introduction

UNRAVELING THE TRUTH

Dida Gazoli

I'd been at a friend's house, at a party near the beach. I was upset by something that happened and decided to leave, but was supposed to sleep over at my friend's house. I took off my shoes and walked on the sand, dipping my feet in the cold, but soothing water. I was about to walk all the way home, a 30-minute trek, when I bumped into one of my brother's friends. Barney was drinking, and likely stoned, but he offered me a ride home. I trusted him more than I did my father, so I got into his car. I told Barney to drop me off up the street, worried his car would wake my parents. I thought I could sneak into the house through the kitchen door, sometimes they forgot to lock it, but I saw the light on. As I reached the door, I could hear my parents arguing. Luckily, the kitchen door was unlocked. My plan was to step inside, dart around the corner, and run upstairs to my bedroom. Later, I'd wish I'd stayed in Barney's car.

"Tell me where you've been, goddamn it!" my father shouted, blocking the closest path to the stairs.

Introduction

UNRAVELING THE TRUTH

Dida Gazoli

I quickly went the other direction, through the kitchen, but he stalked me, pushing me further away from the stairs.

"With Barney," I said. "He drove me home."

"Who the hell's Barney?!"

"Greg's friend," I answered.

"Goddamned Barney!"

"Nothing happened!" I yelled, trying to defend myself, but my father was drunk on rage. He backed me into a corner between a small sofa and the china hutch. I was trapped.

That's when I found out that Mr. Goldenring, the father of my friend whose party it was, called my parents to say I'd gone missing.

"Mr. Goldenring went looking for you, you goddamn tramp! You've ruined the family's reputation!"

My mother pleaded with him, "Frank! Stop! She's home! She's here!"

UNRAVELING THE TRUTH

Dida Gazoli

"You don't give a shit about me!" I shouted. It was the first time I'd ever raised my voice to him or fought back. "You only care about yourself and your reputation!"

Then came the swing. But before his fist connected with my skull, I pulled back and fell into the sofa. In his fumbled punch, he lost his footing and banged into the coffee table; it gave me time to rush past him. I ran, a sprint I'd made many times, upstairs and locked myself in my room. I stormed into the closet, found a gym bag, and started packing. A few minutes later, my mother tried to open my door.

"Please, sweetheart, let me in." I relented, but locked the door after she entered. I headed back to the closet to get more clothes.

"What are you doing?" I heard the panic rise in her voice.

"I'm leaving and going to Jenny's house." Jenny lived nearby and her father was an administrator at the college where my father taught. "And I'm going

UNRAVELING THE TRUTH
Dida Gazoli

to the police," I told her. "I don't have to live like this anymore and neither do you." I was calm and organized in my thinking. I was finally getting out of there. I wasn't going to let what happened to my brothers in high school happen to me. I was doing what my mother hadn't done. My dream of leaving and exposing my father was about to come true. He would finally pay for what he'd done to me and my brothers.

Mama became inconsolable. She knew I had several friends who'd take me in. She knew their parents too, and especially Mr. Goldenring, an attorney, who'd just called to express how concerned he was about my safety. She knew, as did I, that once people found out who my father really was, it would be the loose thread to a full unraveling.

She pleaded and cried like I'd never seen before. Falling apart, she begged me to stay. I didn't want to listen; I wanted to keep to the plan! I'd been building my escape route for so long – *run as fast as you can*

Introduction

UNRAVELING THE TRUTH

Dida Gazoli

– I was a good runner. *Get down the stairs and out the front door. It's not that far -- you can make it!* But Mama kept crying. "Please! I'll talk to him! He'll apologize!" Something my father had never done. "I'll get him to stop! Please, sweetheart!"

Seeing my beautiful mother tormented was excruciating. Her pain and suffering made my body ache, more so than if my father had beaten me. Although my brain didn't want to, my weakened body agreed to stay so she would calm down. But that's when the doubt set in. *You'll make everything worse if you leave. There'll be more pain for her and you. Is that what you want? You're fine. He didn't get you this time. You are fine.* And the gym bag went back into the closet.

I hardly slept that night, and I'm sure my mother didn't. When morning arrived, Dr. Jekyll was back and knocking on my locked door, his voice low and unemotional. "May I come in?" I carefully unlocked the latch and sprang to the opposite side of the

18

UNRAVELING THE TRUTH

Dida Gazoli

bedroom, next to the door of the adjoining room. If he charged at me, I would jump into the spare, guestroom and immediately lock the door. Then I'd climb the steep stairs up to the attic, or further up onto the roof, if I had to. To my utter relief, he remained Jekyll and stayed put in the doorway.

Three words, that's all he could muster, before turning and descending the stairs. "It will change." And it did. I vowed to leave if he or anyone attempted to assault me again. But all the self-esteem I'd felt pumping through my veins hours earlier slowly leaked out of me, and my teenage years spiraled.

I made terrible choices with boyfriends and men in early adulthood, low self-esteem driving my decisions. And when a much older man I dated came after me in a fit of rage, pulling my hair and telling me to get back inside his house, I was afraid if I didn't jump off his carport, some six-seven feet below, he'd pull me back inside and rape me. I landed on the gravel driveway, near my car, but my

UNRAVELING THE TRUTH

Dida Gazoli

left knee buckled and I injured my ligaments. In pain, I limped as fast as I could, got in my car, and got the hell out of there. Gratefully, I'd put my car keys inside my pant pocket, something I still do to this day, because I've trained myself for quick getaways.

As a woman and mother, you may *think* you know what you'd do if you are married to an abuser – but the truth is, it's easy to speculate when you haven't lived that life. Unless you're in a person's mind and body, no one knows what they'll actually do when faced with the same circumstances my mother faced.

Writing this essay reignited my fears, and my father's been gone for 40 years. But fear is a powerful drug that can hold a person's psyche hostage indefinitely. I was afraid to write the truth about the abuse I grew up with because revisiting the memories made them all too real again. I didn't want to go back there. Throughout my adult life, I've tried to make light of the memories or bury them; I wanted

UNRAVELING THE TRUTH

Dida Gazoli

to pretend they weren't *that* bad. For decades, I've tried to find ways to forgive my father for what he did to me and my siblings. I believe that's what my mother did too. She convinced herself that Dr. Jekyll, the best of my father, loved her and us. That may be true, but I've always wanted to expose his abuse, to say his name out loud, and tell people what he did. Because at age 58, I still haven't found a way to escape the memories. They're omnipresent, part of me. However, "telling on him" and revealing what it's like for a child to live in fear inside their own home *does* help to release the pain I've carried for over fifty years.

My mother, as far as I know, only attempted to leave once. And the only time she spoke to me about leaving was to plead with me to stay, because she could never openly talk about the abuse. It was too painful. Too shameful. But it's been eight years since her death, and I no longer have to stay silent to protect her, her feelings, or my family's reputation. I

Introduction

UNRAVELING THE TRUTH

Dida Gazoli

can finally place the blame where it solely belongs, on Frank Maggipinto, my father. Because it's not my or any person's responsibility to protect their abuser. The blue suitcases, the gym bag, and the truth, can finally leave the closet.

Postscript:

While researching why women stay, I've learned how pervasive domestic violence is and that our experience is not unique; women and mothers become steeped in shame and fear, and are often paralyzed by it. They're also estranged from their own families, financially isolated, and totally reliant on the abuser.

Women stay with abusers for many reasons, but "the fear that the abuser's actions will become more violent" tops the list, according to the National Coalition Against Domestic Violence (NCADV); the fear you'll be judged is another main reason women stay. What's wrong with you? How could you love

UNRAVELING THE TRUTH

Dida Gazoli

someone like that? Why didn't you try to leave? The fear of the unknown: Where will I go? How will I feed my kids? The fear of taking your children out of school, a community where they may have positive experiences and stability: It will be even harder to start over. They'll have to make all new friends. And the fear I believe my beautiful mother felt: the truth is so ugly that your appearance and image will be ugly too.

Since writing the final draft of this essay, I learned from my oldest sister that before I was born my mother had also tried* to leave my father. While this hurts, I now understand why it was so difficult, and I can forgive her. Forgiving my father for the pain and fear he inflicted is another story. And one I will save for another volume of *Braving Veracity*.

---

* "On average, it takes a woman 7 attempts to leave an abusive relationship for good." – Jane Clayborne, The James House shelter for domestic violence in Virginia.

INHERITANCE

Sarah Archibald

How do you begin to parse the influence of a man who makes up half of you? You inherited his trauma, his hyper-capable mind, his ability -- no, his *need* -- to escape his heart. This man whose nightly ritual in your Indiana home was to numb the pain with cheap alcohol—Fox Deluxe beer in brown bottles that made a satisfying clink when he dropped another empty one into its slot—and giant bottles of Vino Rosso. On Saturday mornings, you were complicit in turning a donut run into a booze mission, and never asked or even wondered why you always came home with more than breakfast treats.

You didn't know as a kid what pain he harbored, but you sensed it and tried desperately to assuage it. When he came into your room at night, reeking of beer, pungent and overpowering, you'd stare at the tiny pink and green flowers on your wallpaper and escape into your mind, leaving your body behind to endure the abuse. You were there, but you weren't. You learned this from him. He, too, was there and not there, both because he was drunk and because it's common for perpetrators to dissociate,

INHERITANCE

Sarah Archibald

common for them not to remember, making it difficult for him to take responsibility when you confronted him fourteen years ago. You're fifty-two now. You've had extensive therapy in many forms—cognitive behavioral, physical, neurovascular, energetic—and practiced thousands of sun salutations, saying to the Universe with each one that you will take your body back now, thank you. You've thanked your nervous system for its hypervigilant service, told it again and again that you're safe now. And that shrink wrap around your heart? It can come off too, please and thank you.

You were twenty-eight years old the first time you felt anything at all in your heart. You'd just come home from the hospital after giving birth to your first child. You were holding him in a rocking chair, gazing into his tiny, dark eyes, when you felt a surge of energy in your chest. "Ohhhhhhh," you said aloud. "*This* is love!" You'd been pining for it and singing about it since you were a little girl—standing on your play table belting out Olivia Newton John's *Let Me Be There*—but this was your first experience of it. Mind you, you were married,

INHERITANCE

Sarah Archibald

so this realization was both confusing and discombobulating. Your next thought: *If this is love, what am I doing married to Andy?* When you'd met him in your early twenties, you hadn't yet returned to your body, wouldn't return for another decade. He was smart, like you. You had a rapport. He adored you, and you liked being adored, but you wouldn't understand what it's like to adore someone until you'd divorced Andy, continued to heal, returned to your body. You were thirty-eight when you met John, when your heart and the rest of your body were back online, confirming that you wanted him. Consenting, for the first time, with your whole being.

But this relationship, too, was doomed. You loved everything about John, except you didn't love that you couldn't count on him. You didn't love that he sometimes drove his car or rode his bike drunk. You'd fallen in love with John's beautiful soul and thought you had the power to change him. You knew it wasn't a good sign when he called you from his therapist's office and said, "Honey, what are my goals again?" But still you believed you could love him into realizing his potential.

INHERITANCE

Sarah Archibald

You were back in your body, enjoying the hell out of the carnal pleasures the two of you shared, but you'd chosen someone who didn't have the capacity to love you the way you wanted to be loved.

It's what you knew, what felt comfortable, but after twelve years of on-again/off-again, you've finally given up on *what could be* and accepted *what is*. You can see now that each time you grieved what John couldn't give you, you were grieving what your father couldn't give you. *Can't* give you—he's still alive, but you have no contact with him. You haven't been able to reconcile your need to live in your truth, despite your father's denial, and the part of you that wants to tell him you love him before he dies. You aren't even sure if you do love him. Are you afraid to know the answer to that question because you're afraid you don't? Or is it because you're afraid you do love him, and you know he's not capable of loving you back?

You know this: When you were a kid, you loved him desperately. Every weekday afternoon, you'd run down the wooded path behind your house to meet him on his way home from work. "Hi, pal!" he'd say upon seeing

INHERITANCE

Sarah Archibald

you; you were his pal. On the walk, when birds called out, he would answer. You couldn't even whistle, but he would answer them in song. Remembering this forty years later, you realize he was more awake to them than to you, because the moment you reached the house, he'd reach for the bottle.

You understand now that he felt safe in the natural world, but interacting with humans quickly become too much for him. You inherited his reverence for nature, for birds. You have a single tattoo, a swallow, on the underside of your left upper arm. "That bird is definitely flying away," your friend said when you showed it to him. Another voice, a voice from inside, says, *You've spent so much time flying away. Maybe it's time to nest?*

What does it take to nest in this body, your body, a bigger, older version of the body that was repeatedly violated? When you were in sixth grade, you had to quit the trombone you desperately wanted to play because you didn't have the breath for it. When it came time to blow out your birthday candles, you had to get so close that you set your bangs on fire two birthdays in a row. You didn't know then that your lack of lung capacity was

INHERITANCE

Sarah Archibald

tied to the abuse you'd endured, thought it was just one more thing you were bad at. Turns out it was just one more way you assumed fault for something you didn't do. Turns out, when the body is stuck in the sympathetic nervous system—its natural response to stressful situations—it is impossible to breathe properly. You went three decades without exhaling fully.

You carried hypervigilance well into adulthood. Normal, everyday sounds like the furnace working to heat the house, your child showering, or your partner breathing as he fell asleep could turn menacing, firing up your sympathetic nervous system and keeping you from rest, relaxation, and sleep. You felt as though these sounds were being inflicted on you, and you'd cast aspersions in the direction of the offenders rather than recognizing your own hypersensitivity and finding ways to take care of yourself. When your PTSD made you angry or afraid, your behavior drove the people you love away, and when it manifested as shame, self-loathing, or the need to shut down, you had the urge to isolate yourself from others, convincing yourself you despised the people who, in healthier moments, you loved.

INHERITANCE

Sarah Archibald

You're not sure if past is the appropriate tense to use when describing your hypervigilance. You're much, much better, much calmer, but sometimes it comes back. When it does, you write rather than drink. You meditate. Consult cards. Under a full moon, you gather with friends who are new to the world of woo-woo— unconventional beliefs regarded as having little or no scientific basis, especially those relating to spirituality, mysticism, or alternative medicine—to teach them your practice of reading tarot and oracle cards to gain insight into your life. These friends are also new to you, because you've recently moved to Cape Cod from the Midwest, where you lived your whole life but never felt at home. You're an ocean girl—always have been—and waited until you were fifty to live the life you choose. To be reborn. Sort of. You still have the same father. You still share the same surname: Dr. Archibald. When your students at the University of Wisconsin first called you that, you turned and looked behind you. Wondered: *is my father here?* You are the fourth generation of Dr. Archibalds, the first woman, the first to not be named

INHERITANCE

Sarah Archibald

Herb. "Would I have been Herb if I'd been born a boy?" you'd asked him.

"No," he said. "I wouldn't want to burden you with that name."

You understand he didn't *want* to burden you with any of it, that he'd both inherited and experienced pain before you were born and hadn't known how to process it, so he passed it on. But not you. You have metabolized it, released it, written about it. You have endured it, but apart from the genes your kids have inherited. you will not pass it on.

FEMI'S DREAM

Carrie Barcomb

Femi's housewarming party, in the summer of 1997, was a proper affair. The setting sun turned cherry blossoms into pink, twinkling stars that floated above me in the evening breeze and landed on the grass, turning the lawn purple. Walking through the elegant garden blooming with Spring, I stopped to inhale the sweet roses and lavender then adjusted the strap on my black pumps, double-checking my duct-taped heel. I smoothed the wrinkles from my long black dress and took a deep breath before stepping onto the stone path that led to the house. Soon the hum of international languages catapulted me into the mix of sophisticated guests, and I overheard two Englishmen discussing the topiary. "Boxwood is symbolic of immortality," one said.

"Rather, boxwood evokes aristocracy," said the other.

I'd somehow landed on another planet.

I received an invitation to the party because of my brother Alan, a biologist, who was a friend and

FEMI'S DREAM

Carrie Barcomb

colleague of Dr. Akinwole Olufemi Williams, whom most people called Femi.

At 25, I was at a crossroads in my career: should I stay at the well-paying graphic design job in Maryland and continue working for my sexist boss with the peppery mustache, or move to Washington D.C. and accept a government job? Femi was also at a crossroads. A scholarly, Nigerian physician and pathologist, he'd just arrived in the U.S. from London, after being named the first African Scholar-in-Residence at the National Cancer Institute in Maryland. He planned to establish the first comprehensive cancer center in sub-Saharan Africa.

Entering Femi's new home in the suburbs of D.C., I found the sunroom overlooking the pool, and sat down to take it all in. A French diplomat couple walked in and sank into the posh, floral-patterned sofa. The wife sat close to me like we were old friends. The husband grabbed the remote control and turned on the television so he could see the latest news from Spain.

FEMI'S DREAM

Carrie Barcomb

"Bullfighting should be banned!" the wife exclaimed.

The husband quickly countered, "It's an ancient custom we should respect!" which led to a heated argument.

Something inside me decided to pipe up to calm the waters down. "Just because it's a tradition doesn't mean it should continue, especially if it's harmful," I said.

They both turned to me and laughed in agreement. When the screen door slid open, Femi stood there with a bright smile that put everyone at ease. "Thank you for coming!" he said, and asked for us to join him in the dining room. I followed his lead; he carried himself like a dignified king.

A hand-carved cherry table was beautifully set with a buffet of curry and goat-meat dishes, along with French pastries Femi's sister had made. My brother Alan joined us in the dining room, and out of nowhere said, "Dr. Williams wanted to ask if you could help him build a website."

FEMI'S DREAM

Carrie Barcomb

Alan knew I'd had it with my boss in Maryland, and that I was considering a job offer as a webmaster for the Air Force at the Pentagon. However, my boyfriend (now husband) Nate had just accepted a flood-protection job, and was moving to Pennsylvania. Although Alan's question caught me off guard, I looked back and forth between him and Femi and said, "Can you tell me more?"

They explained I could work remotely if I wanted, which offered me the flexibility to join Nate in the mountains along the picturesque Susquehanna River. I immediately said yes. My role would be to present information to global investors of the African Cancer Center (ACC), through brochures and the ACC website.

Soon after the housewarming party, Femi dropped off a box. In his thick Nigerian accent, he said, "Your first task is to scan these photos." They were pictures of untreated pediatric tumors in African children. The children's pained expressions and disfiguring tumors documented a harsh reality I never knew existed.

FEMI'S DREAM

Carrie Barcomb

As a teenager and young adult, I wasn't exactly a stranger to the reality and differences between Black and white communities. Although my white family with European heritage lived near the local Army base, where there was respect for diversity – soldiers don't care much about skin color in life-or-death situations – and I had friends whose families owned farms that served the Underground Railroad, my social-worker mother also wanted me to witness some of the painful realities around me in Baltimore.

One afternoon I'd finished one of my classes at the Maryland Institute College of Art when I noticed Mom's yellow station wagon barreling down Mount Royal Avenue. She veered to the shoulder, and I noticed there was a small child in the back seat.

"Hi, Carrie. Let's take baby Addy to her new home. Then we'll go grocery shopping," Mom said.

As she drove Addy to her foster family, she crossed the boundary between the "good" and "bad" areas of Baltimore, passing neglected rowhouses, boarded-up windows, and chain-link fences. I

FEMI'S DREAM

Carrie Barcomb

adjusted Addy's pink socks while she giggled and looked out the window.

"See that man pushing a stroller, Carrie?" Mom pointed out. "That's not a baby, that's drugs."

We parked along a vacant lot and climbed the steps to a brick rowhouse. The family was welcoming and seemed happy. I talked to the other children and settled Addy into her new high chair. As Mom spoke with the foster mother, I noticed bullet holes inside the concrete walls behind Addy's chair. She cooed and wiggled, her bright eyes full of wonder.

Later, in my senior year of college, I moved to the historic Bolton Hill neighborhood in Baltimore, with its stone churches, family delis, and luxurious brownstones. Friends warned me not to take an apartment near a high-crime area, but I needed an inexpensive rental. The white marble steps leading to the building's front door faced a pristine tree-lined park, but from my bedroom in back, I could hear the nightly *pop pop pop* of gunfire. A local Baltimore psychologist at the time, who was studying the

FEMI'S DREAM

Carrie Barcomb

impact of violence on local children, compared my neighborhood to a war zone.

Then, one day, a friend who lived across the city in a "good" neighborhood, asked, "Doesn't the violence make you hate Black people?"

Did violence make me afraid? Of course. Yet, despite witnessing drive-by shootings and gang violence, I didn't want to live in fear every day. I decided to make eye contact with every Black person I encountered walking down the street. Instead of stereotypical threats, I saw kindness. I saw people restricted by historic, systemic barriers, and I saw that people could still share openness and humanity no matter their race, ethnicity, or gender.

Over the years with Femi, I wanted to talk with him about racism and systemic poverty, but I kept making excuses. I was worried I might say the wrong thing or take up his precious time. One day, he expressed frustration with racist policies rooted in oppressive global history. This led me to say, "I believe learning from Black history helps us all grow."

FEMI'S DREAM

Carrie Barcomb

He didn't look up from his work, but nodded in agreement. The following day he told me about the ACC's building site in Okorisan Village in Lagos, and about the slave port in Badagry. He told the story of the three wells, which represent the three phases of the transatlantic slave trade.

The first is the *Well of Memory Loss,* where slaves were forced to drink to lose their memories of their origins. The second well is called *The Point of No Return,* on nearby Gberefun Island, symbolizing the last step the enslaved would take on native soil. The last is *The Miracle Well,* known for its abundance of clean water, dug when the slave trade flourished. There was hope those enslaved would be freed, and return to this final well to complete the circle.

To heal the wounds of slavery on the African Diaspora, Femi, who'd spent decades researching the divide between Western and African cultures, wanted to return to Nigeria to improve medical infrastructure. He spoke publicly about bridging the gaps in African health care in order to provide

FEMI'S DREAM

Carrie Barcomb

medical treatment comparable to that of developed countries. However, the 2016 U.S. presidential election would delay his return.

The first time I saw Femi angry was after Trump was elected president. African scholars compared Trump to African dictators. Femi explained that Africans were fed up with corrupt politicians, saying, "In the Shona language: *zvakwana*; in Ndebele: *sokwanele,* and in English: *enough is enough.*"

Trump's presidency signaled a halt to the African Cancer Center's Western funding. Femi cited American filmmaker and historian Ken Burns's description of how African Americans continue to be pushed to the back of the line. Femi's plans to complete once-attainable goals, such as "equipment donation and cobalt for radiotherapy procurement," were no longer on his to-do list, with notations like, "under Trump, this may be very difficult," or, "now impossible."

Meanwhile, an overwhelming number of African citizens continued to suffer and die from cancer. Nigeria had only seven radiotherapy machines, and five were faulty. This meant one radiotherapy machine for every 20 million people. Femi's proposed African Cancer Center would have provided treatment for an estimated 200 million people.

Most of the time, Femi and I shared project details via email. Though he kept his feelings close, the subject lines of his emails often reflected his mood or thoughts. When our team faced challenges, he sent uplifting messages to boost our spirits. The subject line of one email was *The Joy and Future of ACC*, and in the body of the email he shared a quote by theology professor Lewis Smedes: "You and I were created for joy, and if we miss it, we miss the reason for our existence!" I looked forward to his emails of hope. Our team longed to see this project built, and I prayed every day that Femi would see the ACC completed.

That year he began sharing with me more and more personal photos and stories from his life, including his childhood, along with emails entitled, "Exactly one month after my birthday today," and

FEMI'S DREAM

Carrie Barcomb

"The question is counting down or counting up?" Then he sent, "Shockingly accurate ways to predict your death," and "Famous Last Words." *Was he sick? I didn't feel it was my place to ask.*

In January of 2017, Femi finally reported some good news. A South African hospital-management company was awarded a contract for Phase 1 of ACC's pre-construction development. By June, he sent more good news: "Money to build is on the way." There was a sense of relief as construction moved forward.

Six months later, Femi turned 85, and I was happy to hear he was given a clean bill of health and the green light to return to Nigeria to oversee ACC construction. Things were on track, and he asked me to post his upcoming research paper, which he would later present in Rwanda, on the ACC website.

A week later, my brother called. "Sad news, Carrie," Alan said. "Femi wasn't feeling well, and called an ambulance, but he passed away before it arrived."

FEMI'S DREAM

Carrie Barcomb

I was breathless. Then a colleague delivered another devastating blow: "ACC construction cannot continue."

For over two decades, I'd carried the hope of Femi's dream. Throughout his lifetime, he'd dedicated himself to alleviating the suffering of millions of people. He was a brilliant man, and many things to many people: doctor, teacher, scholar, activist, mentor, colleague. To me, he was a beacon of light, who looked for the positive in others with unwavering perseverance and a sense of duty, no matter the difficulties he faced. It was an honor to be a part of that legacy. He once told me, "Find purpose in joy, Carrie," and, "The greatest joys in life come from family, friendship, and participation in the community."

On February 13, 2022, my email inbox was painfully empty, but I still had a dozen or so unopened messages from Femi. Perhaps I kept them for a rainy day, or maybe it was my peculiar way of keeping his memory and work alive. One of them was titled *Dream*. When I finally opened it, there was

Carrie Barcomb

no message. I still have three more emails from him, but I don't think I'll open them. Their titles are enough: *Laughter is the Best Medicine, Positive Thoughts for Your Day*, and *Keep Going.*

Postscript:

On February 14, 2022, I received this message from the Chairman of the African Cancer Center, Adekunle Olumide: "Today is indeed a milestone in the history of the ACC project, which has been on the runway for some time, waiting to take off. It is with immense pleasure that I welcome you all to the signing ceremony, appointing financial advisors for the African Cancer Center. It was the background of poor cancer management in Nigeria that led to the establishment of the center by the late Professor Olufemi Williams, Founder and Director of the African Cancer Center."

The Nigerian national anthem states: *The labor of our heroes past shall never be in vain.* Femi's dedication to his dream inspired me to reach beyond my own boundaries. It not only changed the

FEMI'S DREAM

Carrie Barcomb

trajectory of my career, but my life, and I learned that
no matter our differences, we can create meaningful
connections to build something greater than
ourselves.

***

GIFTED

Jamila Beale

My four-year-old son Will was dragging his feet, and the last place I wanted to be was at Giant supermarket on a Saturday afternoon. Luckily, I just needed two more things on our list and we could check out. I took Will's hand to hurry him up, and he froze.

"What does 'nigger' mean?" he asked.

Surely, I'd misheard him. But then he repeated the question even louder. It hit me like a bucket of ice-cold water.

A white couple who stood nearby stared at us and began to whisper. An older white woman shook her head with a *humph*. Instead of being empathetic, they were passing judgment. I wanted to say, "He didn't learn it from me."

We don't use that word in my home. For some other Black Americans, the variant ending in 'a' is a term of endearment, and it symbolizes a shared history. It's not used in a derogatory way when Black Americans use it with one another, but it's still

Jamila Beale

controversial, so I prefer not to use it at all. I stooped down to Will's level. "Where did you hear that?"

"The boys said it." I'd seen two white teenagers standing nearby, but when Will turned around to point them out, they were gone.

The first time I was called the n-word was in Aberdeen, Maryland, in 2012. I had expected it to happen in State College, Pennsylvania, where I went to college. My dad warned me to be careful. He was worried about me living in a white rural town where the Klan was rumored to exist.

I hadn't experienced racism directly, but in 2006, during my sophomore year at Penn State, a student yelled from their dorm window at the Black Caucus president as he walked by: "I'm going to lynch all you niggers off campus!"

Afterward, I participated in student-led protests in front of Old Main, the building where the president's office was. Hundreds of us gathered and urged the university to take action against the student who committed the act. Penn State, or rather the Board of Trustees, voted not to pursue disciplinary

GIFTED

Jamila Beale

action, but instead encouraged the community to have more dialogue concerning race and diversity. We were disappointed, but not defeated. We reflected on the perseverance of Calvin H. Waller and Mildred S. Bunton, the first Black male and female graduates of Penn State, and their determination to graduate and diversify the school. We students felt it was our duty to recruit more Black scholars and encourage them to leave campus with a diploma in hand. I developed strength and perseverance at Penn State, and six years later those attributes would further my self-confidence.

I was living in Aberdeen with my fiancée and our dog Seven. There was a park ten minutes from our apartment. One cool spring morning, I told my fiancé I would take Seven out for a walk, but left my phone at home. I hadn't planned to stay long. The grass sparkled with dew as Seven and I walked, pausing every so often to birdwatch and smell the fresh air. No one else was in the field that morning, and aside from the infrequent sound of a passing car, all was quiet and peaceful until we moved closer to the

Jamila Beale

roadway, and a man screamed, "Nigger, get out of here!" from his car window.

Those words landed like a slap across my face. Three white men were sitting in a doorless Jeep, laughing. Armed with nothing but a leash and a twelve-pound Puggle, I couldn't even phone my dad or fiancé. The men eventually sped away, wheels squealing, the American flag waving from the back of the Jeep, and I thought, *America is my home. I am not leaving.* Seven and I ended our walk with a victory lap.

In both of those situations, I wasn't a mother yet. In the supermarket with my son, there would be no protests or victory laps because this was about protecting Will.

Well before Will's kindergarten class made him their "little mayor," he shook hands and talked with people. He'd initiate a conversation with a stranger anytime. "Hi, my name is Will," he'd say. "What's your name?"

I was often the third wheel, a bodyguard, or invisible. But there were occasions when someone

Jamila Beale

who praised Will for his speaking abilities also acknowledged me. He made lasting first impressions.

"Hello, Will," a woman said one afternoon when we were in line at a popular creamery. "Looking forward to getting some ice cream?" Will waved, but I had no clue who she was; then she told me she'd spoken with him at a playground the previous month.

"Next, he'll be giving strangers his birthdate and address," I told my husband.

"Will's just friendly," he responded. "Don't worry."

But I did worry. Watching him talk with people beyond a greeting made me uncomfortable. I was raised to not talk to strangers, for obvious reasons, but Will's openness and friendly nature toward strangers was a gray zone to me. Should I set boundaries? Put an end to it?

I decided to coach him before we entered a store. "Listen, Mommy needs to get in and out today. We can chat with the cashier another day." Then I incorporated the book *Don't Talk to Strangers* by

GIFTED

Jamila Beale

Christine Mehlhaff into his nighttime routine. However, none of this stopped him from talking to any person who'd listen.

Until that moment in the supermarket, I had accepted Will's personality and intelligence as his gifts, but now I harbored some resentment. *Maybe this wouldn't have happened if he wasn't so friendly. We can't be naïve. People can be unkind and fake.*

Then I stopped myself mid-thought. *No! He didn't ask for this! He's a friendly, kind, curious boy. Why can't Black people just live their lives?* Will hadn't faltered. His gifts were pure. He was still confident, undeterred, and truthful, but I was unprepared. I hadn't planned to teach a lesson on racial prejudice while buying groceries, but the least I could do was answer Will's question honestly. "Nigger means ignorant, stupid," I explained.

Will looked lost, trying to make sense of it all. I didn't lie, but I also didn't tell him the word's origin, how it was used to humiliate and dehumanize our ancestors, our great-great grandparents. Then I blamed myself for letting it happen. *You should have*

Jamila Beale

been standing next to him! The boys who used the word were about the same age as the Jackson, Mississippi teens who pled guilty to a federal hate crime in the murder of James Craig Anderson. Like Mr. Anderson, Will was targeted because of his race, and because he was defenseless. Would the boys have said the same thing to me? I wanted to find out.

I frantically searched all twelve aisles like I was looking for a missing child. When I didn't see the boys, I thought they might be at the cash registers, about to leave the store. My heart and my legs carried me quickly to the checkout lines, and I gripped Will's little fingers. I couldn't see anything beyond confronting those boys and whoever else was involved.

"Do you see them?" I repeatedly asked Will.

"There they are," he said.

But I couldn't find them. I couldn't *see* them. It was as if God shielded me from the embarrassment and I avoided a trap, an attempt to make a video of me yelling, with the store manager running behind me, waving his hands in the air, and telling me to

GIFTED

Jamila Beale

"leave, or I'll call the cops." They could have posted it online with hashtags like #AngryBlackFemale or #BadMomAward. But that is not my story. My internal voice rose above the noise around me. It said *breathe. It's okay.* Then I heard Will's voice. "Mommy," he said, tugging on my arm, "I'm here. Just two more things to get and we'll leave."

Being a mother is like being an emotional encyclopedia. Usually, we can reference the answers right away. Other times, we go with our gut. I can't protect my son from racial hatred; he doesn't live in a bubble or a vacuum. He will have his heart broken, fall out with friends, and experience grief, just like the rest of us. But I *can* prepare him for life in America by sharing my experiences and providing sound advice. I can teach him how to fight systemic racism with pen and paper. My presence can be a source of comfort and refuge. I'll encourage him to seek out education and Black authors like Richard Wright and James Baldwin, and he'll learn about Freddie Gray and Trayvon Martin. We'll laugh at ignorance and celebrate Black culture and

GIFTED

Jamila Beale

achievements.   And   above   all,   my   son
will love despite hate.

***

*Four years after that afternoon in Giant, I shared
this story with Will. He cried, not from being called
a racial slur but from the thought that Mommy can't
live forever. I love you, Will.*

SUMMER OF THE CARP

Catherine Braik-Selin

Another sweltering summer day mercifully releases its chokehold on the Delaware Valley. My car rolls into the city of Wilmington just as the last wisps of sun-burnished clouds go dark. I turn left at the Citgo gas station where a low-rider with tinted windows pumps gas to thrums of pulsating bass notes. Rounding the corner, I see flashing lights. Police again. Thankfully, I find a parking space and maneuver my small car into a spot across from my front door; I live in one of the few single-family residences on the block. I'm proud of my turn-of-the-century home, with its stately white pillars and sturdy brick facade, a house that would cost twice as much just a few blocks away, on the other side of Concord Pike, where the demographics flip to white middle class.

My neighbors congregate in multi-generational groups on their front porches, stoops, and stairways. They're talking over each other and angling for a better view of the action, as bursts of red and blue

Catherine Braik-Selin

ricochet off windows and car mirrors. Cones of white light from police flashlights penetrate the narrow, dark alleyways.

"What's going on?" I ask Monica.

"We heard gunfire down on 25th Street," she says, her head tipped in the direction of the disturbance. Like many neighbors on my block, Monica is a single mom trying to raise a Black son. "Thank God TJ is home tonight," she murmurs, her voice trailing off as she imagines a different scenario. My body shudders and a flashback of George surfaces: he's standing at the back door of my childhood home in New Jersey, holding a crumpled paper bag. After more than fifty years, America is still a dangerous place for people of color and men like George and TJ.

I turn to Monica and say, "You're doing a great job, 'Mom.'"

"It ain't easy, Miss Catherine," she answers, "but honest-to-God, I don't know what I'd do without him. Did I tell you he got a job at a recording studio?"

SUMMER OF THE CARP

Catherine Braik-Selin

"TJ told me last week! He seemed really pumped."

"You know, I thought those online COVID courses would knock all the fire out of him. But finally, he's following his dream."

I keep watch from the front porch, rocking slowly in my chair until the last police car cruises down the street. Only then can I breathe a sigh of relief. There are no casualties, this time. Gradually, folks settle back on their porches or stoops and turn up the music: Freestyle rap across the street, cool Motown around the corner, and Latin pop a few doors down. Adolescent boys circle the block on their bikes, popping wheelies, and someone fires up their backyard grill. Soon the primal scent of sizzling meat blends with the acrid smoke from back alley spliffs passing hands. I'm suddenly ravenous.

Back inside my kitchen, I rummage through my refrigerator. I won't go to bed hungry tonight, or any other night. I'm keenly aware of the privileges I enjoy due to the color of my skin. And again and again, I see George standing at the back door holding

Catherine Braik-Selin

the paper bag, his green pickup idling in the driveway. *It was the summer of the carp:* 1967, my father confined to his bed, struggling to breathe.

***

Mama hit the bottle hard on Friday nights. The noisy air conditioner that kept Father comfortable upstairs in their bedroom could almost drown out the quarrels that were commonplace when she drank. On the weekends, my little brother Charlie and I would sneak downstairs before Mama awakened. We'd run outside to play, confident she wouldn't even notice we were gone.

The morning that rings in my mind like church bells began with a sputtering cacophony of unknown origin. When the dust and puffs of dandelion settled on our grassy driveway, I saw an old green pick-up heaped with broken chairs, scrap metal, and burlap sacks. The truck slowed to a stop outside our dining room window. A collection of rakes, shovels, and assorted tools were lined up against the cab's window, vertically bisecting the glass. The house windows rattled, then stopped the instant the

SUMMER OF THE CARP

Catherine Braik-Selin

mysterious stranger cut the engine. Charlie and I
peered through the sheer curtains and made out a face
between rows of tools. He looked like a cartoon
character behind bars. All he needed was a suit with
stripes like the crooks wear on *Looney Tunes*.

The truck door swung open, and I told Charlie,
"Quick! Hide!" As I grabbed hold of the curtains and
pulled them tightly around us, the rod snapped in half
and hit Charlie squarely on the head. He bawled, and
Mama charged down the stairs, yelling, "Now, what
are you two up to?" Her thin brown hair stuck out in
all directions, and her bloodshot eyes looked
magnified behind her cat-eye glasses.

Tap, tap, tap. The stranger was at the back door.
Mama admonished us to "pipe down," then walked
to the small kitchen, muttering, "Who the hell is it?"
Charlie and I extricated ourselves from the musty
curtains and ran to catch a glimpse of the man. Mama
smoothed her hair back and cinched her robe around
her narrow frame before opening the back door.

Standing on the stoop was a slightly built man,
neatly dressed in worn trousers and a light jacket. His

face was warm and lined with age. His brown cheeks were somewhat hollow, his eyes dark and bright, but also tired and sad. He briefly caught my eye and swept off his hat, holding it across his chest.

"Are you the lady of the house?" he asked.

"Yes, yes," Mama said. "How can I help you?"

"My name is George, and I wonder… do you folks need any work done around the place?"

"Oh my," Mama replied, "is there anything that *doesn't* need fixing around here? These two little monsters just broke my curtain rod, and who knows what else they'll be getting into!"

George's kind voice mesmerized me. I stood there, staring idiotically, because he looked so different from everybody else in town. He was also the shyest grownup I'd ever encountered. As he and Mama talked, Charlie whipped around and ran out the front door, with me close on his heels. But later that morning, I grew tired of minding my baby brother, and left Charlie with his toy trucks in the dirt, under the old maple tree where Mama could see him from the kitchen. I sprinted for the apple tree at

SUMMER OF THE CARP

Catherine Braik-Selin

the edge of our yard, near the woods, pigtails flying. In my pocket was a copy of *Winnie the Pooh*, my favorite book. I climbed up to a sturdy branch and nestled into its hollow, quickly losing myself in the adventures of Christopher Robin.

Bang! I nearly slipped. *Is Joey O'Brien throwing rocks again?* Joey was a big bully. But when I looked down, I was relieved to see George. He was dumping a wheelbarrow full of sticks at the edge of the woods. He pulled a faded, blue handkerchief from his pocket, wiped his brow, and headed off for another load. In that moment, George had no idea I was perched in the apple tree, and I had no idea how indispensable he would become to my family.

Before Father got sick, he tended a big garden full of wondrous things. He walked shirtless in the midday sun, with a constellation of freckles glistening beneath a sheen of sweat on his back, and I followed along behind him and filled my bucket with weeds he left piled between rows of plantings. Father would methodically raise the hoe and thrust it back into the earth. Learning the names of the plants

SUMMER OF THE CARP

Catherine Braik-Selin

gave me great pleasure, more than the actual eating of the vegetables and fruits Father planted: squash, rutabagas, kohlrabi, rhubarb, Swiss chard, cherry tomatoes. Lifting a broad low leaf, velvety smooth on top and prickly underneath, I might find a knobby fruit no larger than a newborn kitten.

"Look, Father! Look what I found!"

"That, Cathy, is a patty pan squash," he explained. Stretching out his calloused hands, he promised, "We can pick it when it's this big."

And Charlie, from his nearby playpen, mimicked me as I stretched out my hands. "*This big!*" he repeated.

Seasons passed, and George continued to show up at our back door. My mother always found something in need of fixing or hauling. I never questioned why he didn't come to the front door. But in the 1960s, and of course hundreds of years before that, a Black man didn't show up unannounced at white folks' homes.

The garden eventually became overrun with pests that nibbled their way through root, leaf, and

SUMMER OF THE CARP

Catherine Braik-Selin

vine. Father tried to keep up, but he frequently got overheated and short of breath. I'd bring him icy tumblers of lemonade and warm chocolate chip cookies, which we shared under the shade of the maple tree. Then a big storm split our beloved tree in two. One ragged half fell across our garden with a thunderous crash, destroying what few vegetables had survived that punishing season. By that point, Father seemed to have given up, and Charlie and I spent hours climbing through the jungle of limbs and leaves reenacting scenes from *Swiss Family Robinson*. Winter arrived and blanketed the garden with snow early that year, turning the leafy canopy of the downed maple into a snug fort, where Charlie and I hunkered down with mugs of hot cocoa clutched between our mittens.

When George returned after the final spring thaw, his first job was to dismantle that messy tree, limb by limb, with a handsaw. "It's a damned eyesore!" we heard Mama tell George.

"But Mama, that's our fort!" we pleaded, to no avail.

SUMMER OF THE CARP

Catherine Braik-Selin

"Stand back there, sugar," George warned me in his soft Southern drawl, cutting the branches and piling them up at the edge of the garden. He let me cart off armloads of sticks in a wheelbarrow to dump at the edge of the woods. When George was finally finished, he gathered up his tools in his ramshackle truck and said, "Thank you, Little Miss," before driving home.

Did George have a family and children of his own? I imagine he did, yet I only knew him as the man with the green truck and the kind heart, much like my father whose name was also George.

I was nine the following spring, when I watched the father I once knew fade away. George performed all the jobs Father could no longer do. And even though money was tight, we relied on George more than ever, with Father tethered to his bed and oxygen tank. My mother was forced to quit her job to care for him full-time, and my family fell into abject poverty.

By summer, the inevitable happened. George knocked at the kitchen door like he normally did, but

SUMMER OF THE CARP

Catherine Braik-Selin

this time Mama admitted the truth. "We can't afford to pay you anymore, George. My husband is terribly sick, but he asked me to thank you for everything you've done for us. We're very sorry to let you go."

"Ma'am," George replied, "I surely am sorry to hear this. Just let me finish trimming up that hedge today – you don't owe me nothing. I'll keep your family in my prayers."

The next week, George's green truck pulled into the driveway again, followed by his familiar knock at the back door. He held a crumpled brown bag. I ran upstairs to get Mama. But by the time she came to the door George was backing out of the driveway. On the stoop sat the fragrant bag, surrounded by our excited brood of cats: Nimbus, Stripey, Deirdre, and my father's favorite, Schrödinger, whose name was a curiosity to me.

Mama lifted the bag and opened it. There, wrapped in newspaper, was a freshly caught carp. The old saying "hunger is the best sauce" is apt. But George's generosity and Mama's skill in the kitchen ensured that, although we were often hungry, we

SUMMER OF THE CARP

Catherine Braik-Selin

never went to bed hungry. Sober or not, she dished out a fine supper. With boiled potatoes, herbs, a light cheese sauce, or stewed tomatoes and creamed corn, she managed to thread enough flavors in with the carp to sate her children's appetites. There were more carp to follow, occasionally accompanied by a bag of tomatoes or zucchini. Each week, and all summer long, we could rely on at least one carp dinner thanks to George. He never failed to ask about Father when he stopped by, and Father always asked after George from his sickbed.

I have since learned that carp are remarkable fish. They can survive for great lengths of time with little to no oxygen, whether in the frigid depths of winter or in high summer. The memory of carp and its power to sustain my family in desperate times continues to swim beneath the currents of my life. I also recently learned about Erwin Schrödinger, a Nobel Prize winning Austrian physicist and colleague of Einstein. "Schrödinger's cat" was a quantum physics thought experiment: "In quantum mechanics lingo, the cat's ability to be both alive and

SUMMER OF THE CARP

Catherine Braik-Selin

dead until it is observed is referred to as 'quantum indeterminacy' or the observer's paradox."

Although my parents are both gone, I can bring them back with a concerted act of recollection and observation. I'm comforted by my own "observer's paradox," and sometimes imagine Father sitting with me on my front porch in Wilmington. Gracie, my tuxedo cat, is on my lap; Schrödinger is in my father's.

"Schrödinger," I muse with a chuckle. How I cherish the thought that my parents shared this inside joke before our world was torn apart. In my imagined Saturday afternoon, Father's feet are no longer swollen in his tan slippers – his eyes are bright, his cheeks rosy, and he's breathing just fine. Charlie and Mama are with us too, but she isn't drinking. Instead of sherry, there's a bottle of quinine on the porch table. The sparkling liquid glitters like crystal in the midday sun, and a plate of my gooey chocolate chip cookies sweetens the languid summer air. We're talking about what to make for dinner: baked pattypan squash, roasted chicken and cucumber

Catherine Braik-Selin

salad, maybe Lazy Daisy Cake for dessert. Monica and TJ arrive just as George pulls up in his green truck in front of the house. This time, he doesn't hesitate to walk right up the front steps. With a wink, he asks me, "Are you the lady of the house?"

"I surely am, Mr. George."

"Had a good run of brook trout this morning," he tells Father. "Going to have us a fish fry tonight!"

"George!" Father exclaims, shaking off a surprised Schrödinger, and walking over to greet his friend. "Sorry we didn't make it down to the river today. Cathy needed help with her cookies!" He passes George the plate.

"I could smell 'em from my truck!"

The neighborhood boys are showing off, popping wheelies in the middle of the intersection. They toss their bikes onto the grass and clamber up the steps, taking two at a time. "Don't worry," I say, "There's plenty left. And Mr. George, I saved an extra big batch for you and your family."

***

SUMMER OF THE CARP

Catherine Braik-Selin

Cathy's Bittersweet Chocolate Chunk Cookies

Preheat oven to 350°

Baking Time 13 - 15 minutes

1 ½ cups flour

½ tsp. baking soda

½ tsp. salt

1 stick unsalted butter, browned* and cooled

1 ¼ cup dark brown sugar, lightly packed

1 ½ tsp. vanilla extract

1 large egg, plus 1 egg yolk

4 - 5 oz. bar bittersweet or semi-sweet chocolate,
broken into chunks

♦ Sift together the flour, baking soda and salt into
a medium bowl and set aside.

♦ Cream the butter and sugar on low speed until
smooth.

♦ Add the vanilla, egg and egg yolk and beat on
low speed until fully incorporated. Do not
overbeat.

SUMMER OF THE CARP

Catherine Braik-Selin

♦ Add the flour mixture in stages and beat just until incorporated. Scrape down the sides of the bowl. Add the chocolate chunks and mix with a wooden spoon until evenly distributed.

♦ Adjust oven racks to lower and upper thirds of oven. Line two baking sheets with parchment paper. Spoon the dough into golf ball sized portions. Batter should make approximately 12 cookies.

♦ Bake for 13 - 15 minutes or until golden brown around the edges, turning the sheets front to back and switching racks halfway through. Remove from the oven and put hot cookies on a cooling rack to let cool and settle.

♦ To brown butter, melt over medium low heat in a silver or light-colored saucepan. Butter will melt and pop, then begin to change color. Swirl pan. Butter will begin to smell nutty and should be removed from heat when it's caramel in color, about 3 - 5 minutes.

Catherine Braik-Selin

♦ Place brown butter in a large mixing bowl to cool before adding the rest of the ingredients, about 20 - 30 minutes.

***

Lazy Daisy Cake

Beat until thick: 2 eggs

Gradually add: 1 cup sugar

1 tsp. vanilla

Add: 1 tsp. baking powder

¼ tsp salt

1 cup flour

♦ Heat to boiling point: ½ cup milk & 1 tsp. butter

♦ Add to previous mixture, beating well. (Batter is thin, but do not add more flour.)

♦ Pour batter into greased 8" square tin and bake in 350° oven for 30 minutes.

♦ Remove from oven and spread with, in the following order:

3 tbs. soft butter

SUMMER OF THE CARP

Catherine Braik-Selin

5 tbs. brown sugar

2 tbs. cream

½ cup shredded coconut

Put under broiler until coconut is golden brown.

Watch carefully!

CORNERSTONES

Elle Fern

At midlife, I realized it was time to examine the life I'd built and face the architect. From an outsider's point of view, I checked all the boxes of a "successful" woman: I was married to a loving man, and had two beautiful children and a cozy suburban home. But I was running from an anxiety so deep I barely recalled a life without it.

I imagine many former Christians share this anxiety, those of us raised "in the church" who decide to leave it. My departure at age 20 was unceremonious. After a life of Christian school and church ideology, I simply ceased participating, attending, and forcing myself to believe. But my anxiety didn't cease. It grew.

Stories of hell first ignited my fears as a child. A wrong choice could cast me into hell's fiery pit for all eternity, continually burned alive. Bible class, chapel, and Sunday services reinforced my sinful nature, my hopelessness, and my profound need for absolution. Shame made itself a home in my spirit.

CORNERSTONES

Elle Fern

Then "evangelical purity" reached a dizzying crescendo, teaching me that my body was not my own; it was meant for someone else's eyes, pleasure, and control. I graduated from Christian school and met the secular world with great unease.

Although I'd turned away from evangelical ideologies as a 20-year-old, they continued to complicate my sense of self over the next two decades. An eating disorder and alcohol helped to numb my mind for a time. Achievements and box-ticking also provided some fulfillment. And raising my children restored me in incalculable ways. Yet, at midlife, I awakened some days crying and hardly able to breathe, with pieces of myself missing. Tired of the vise in my chest, I began to search for answers to questions about the world I'd left twenty years earlier. I turned to authors and thinkers. Podcasts, books, and blogs soon replaced cabernet and Netflix. That's when I met James Baldwin.

Cozy in my bedroom, with my kids occupied and my husband practicing music, I read Baldwin's semi-autobiographical novel *Go Tell It on the Mountain.*

CORNERSTONES

Elle Fern

John Grimes, Baldwin's main character, lives in a tense home ruled by a stepfather who looms monstrously, but basks in honor as pastor of their church, which makes his domestic power and cruelties seem even more stark. Grimes' mind wanders throughout the novel, vacillating between the narrow community of his church, which includes his family; and the world outside this bubble, whose warmth calls to him. The novel ends with Grimes overcome by the Holy Spirit, flinging himself headlong into the church, just as a young Baldwin did.

***

"I supposed Him to exist only within the walls of a church—in fact, of our church—and I also supposed that God and safety were synonymous."

– James Baldwin,

Down at The Cross:

Letter from a Region of My Mind (1962)

Every Sunday at Cornerstone Church, my family sat in the back corner, where my father recorded

CORNERSTONES

Elle Fern

every sermon on cassette tape and took copious notes. He was in constant motion. My mother was the inverse, upright and rapt for the sermon's duration, then lively and engaging afterwards, presenting the pastor with theological challenges he refused to discuss with her at length. There was no room, or time, for debate.

I was angular and edgy, all cheekbones, nose, and darting eyes, a cygnet aspiring to be a full-grown swan. I knew that in order to belong, I had to be pretty, thin, and demure, but I wasn't sure I'd achieve it. On Sunday mornings, I armored myself in the heavy varsity coat I'd managed to acquire from The Gap, the V-neck sweater I'd stolen from my dad's closet, a black pencil skirt, and Payless ballet flats. I'd slink into our back pew for the weekly sermon, lean my body against the cool plaster white wall, and count the minutes. If Pastor Dave was giving the sermon, we'd end on time at 11:30; if it was Pastor Doug, who moonlighted as an amateur comedian and was the most talkative person I knew, we'd be there until noon. I'd turn and steal glances at the clock

CORNERSTONES

Elle Fern

during hymns or the occasional stretch, and the minute hand stared back, hardly moving.

Dave was the head pastor at Cornerstone and our primary conduit to the Lord. He was adored by both the men and women of the congregation. He resembled the high school football star he'd once been, with a strong jaw; muscular arms; and a pressed, taut shirt stretched across his chest. In the receiving line after church, his megawatt smile turned on as we congratulated him on another job well done. When his wife passed away from cancer at an early age, the line of bachelorettes was long. He selected Mickie, whose sincere adoration was unmatched, and she helped look after Dave's three children, all teenagers like me.

Pastor Dave's daughter, Gretchen, was the epitome of beauty in my eyes, with thick auburn hair and the brown eyes of a doe. She was cheerful when elders spoke to her, and demure in her long, flowery dresses. She sat quietly near her brothers as her father preached. I mentally flew around the room, tracing the jewel-toned stained-glass windows with my eyes,

77

Elle Fern

smoothing wrinkles from the blood-red carpet, and studying Gretchen. She possessed an unshakable belonging, embraced by the inner sanctum, while I watched from its periphery. My family felt like sloppy Christians, yelling at each other on the way to church, sitting awkwardly at potlucks, and in need of every bit of affirmation we could get. Gretchen's echelon felt out of reach.

Although Pastor Dave ran the show, there were sometimes guest speakers. One particular Sunday, we heard from Peg, a long-time churchgoer like us. As she stood to make her way to the pulpit, her pew creaked in relief, or perhaps warning. Pastor Dave waited for her to climb the carpeted stairs and take his place at the pulpit, arms at his sides like a sentry. I'd been up there before when no one was looking. I'd seen Pastor Dave's pencils and notes in their podium shelf, and the snakepit of microphone wires tangled below, hidden from view. And I'd peered out at the congregation, like Peg was about to do, and seen the holy diorama from that God-like view.

CORNERSTONES

Elle Fern

I liked Peg. She was kind and garrulous, "too much" by many social measures, and she carried extra weight and spoke with extra volume. She was friendly to everyone. In church, she channeled her "too-muchness" into a fierce, abiding reverence for the words of the pastors, clapping or whooping in agreement from her pew up front. But that Sunday, Peg's heart was broken. Cancer had snatched her husband Ron from her. Beside her in the pew was a gaping void where Ron had once sat, with Peg's gentle arm draped around his back. Peg's grief was fresh as she slowly described Ron's suffering. The church was their inner sanctum. It was where their boys, often troublesome, fell into step. It was where Peg taught Vacation Bible School, donated hand-me-downs, and cooked up casseroles that the church men hungrily swooped upon after baptisms and barbecues. It was where Peg assumed she had listeners.

She climbed to the pulpit and looked out at us. With tearful strokes, she painted a picture of a life lost too soon. She described how she'd made Ron

Elle Fern

broth when he couldn't eat. How she'd washed his limbs. Peg waded in a river of catharsis until she was swept away, allowing the current to carry her.

I watched Pastor Dave's face as he sat in the velvet, tufted chair behind her. His brow was wrinkled. Peg was going on too long. This widow's life was beginning to impose on the congregation's day, her river of grief flooding our space. Pastor Dave had a whole flock to think of, many of whom fixed their pleading eyes on him. My father shifted in his pew, but my mother's eyes glistened with tears. I, for once, was patient and open to hearing what Peg needed to tell us. She described the pain that ran through her husband's limbs, miming how she'd rubbed his legs to soothe his pain.

"Thank you, Peg," Pastor Dave finally said, standing up, his eyes on the congregation. It was time to move on. Peg's arms fell, but she nodded in agreement and descended the pulpit stairs.

Something shifted in me then. I sensed a charade, a paradox, a great black chasm between the "righteous" words we read, sang, and swallowed

Elle Fern

whole, and the things we did. Pastor Dave and the congregation could not - would not - carry the grief of a widow. We would not sacrifice twenty extra minutes for Peg's destroyed life.

After the service, my parents debated what happened, circling our kitchen without looking at each other. They often discussed the morning's sermon in a spirited conversation, but that day the mood was heavy. My mother was furious. "She was right in the middle...he shouldn't have done that." She was used to Pastor Dave's cordial silencing, but watching him deal such a blow to someone so vulnerable, before the whole congregation, was new.

"He had to do it," my father asserted with a shrug, as if it were obvious. Although that was the final word, it didn't ring true to me or my mother. Another resentment stored, but not forgotten. If Peg couldn't fall apart in church, with us, her Christian community, her brothers and sisters in faith, then where could she fall apart? Was there any place more apt than her church?

CORNERSTONES

Elle Fern

"I can't believe what you say,
because I see what you do."
– J. Baldwin

Over time, I began to see the pulpit as a strange place. In its presence, I shrank, averting my eyes. I could not respond with love to the men who stood there, pleading for our captive attention, our worship, our obedience. My role in the church was to abide quietly, to accept as divine the words of men. But if there was one hole in a framework claiming to be absolute, there might as well be a million. Time after time, I witnessed ruthless rejection of the weak in my religious community, tiny cracks that spiderwebbed through the mirage of solid ground. Widows abandoned and silenced. Pregnant young women shunned and rejected, while the boys who got them pregnant breezed on by. Trusted male teachers flirting with students when no one was watching. I saw the strong male athletes and lithe pretty girls exalted, and the vulnerable cast aside.

CORNERSTONES

Elle Fern

Leaving religion as a young adult is like blowing up the only bridge back home. Everything must be reworked, reconfigured, a feat of mental gymnastics in a new, strange land. So much of my identity was gone, and I'd taken no time to rebuild it. Fundamentalism answered looming questions when I was a child, but those questions were uncapped and raw when I was 20. *What happens when you die? Where do we come from? What is the point of all of this?* My answers, so clear before, vanished. After a lifetime of grooming steeped in black and white, it felt unsafe to face the gray. Instead, I took off running and tried not to look back. Over the next decade or so, my feet barely met the ground. College, love, marriage, and babies provided me a stairwell to climb and a place to hide. But we can only hide for so long.

I returned to Cornerstone Church many years later for my father's second marriage. Still at the helm of Cornerstone, Pastor Dave presided. After the ceremony, I spoke with his wife Mickie about their family, the children I'd grown up with. Around the

Elle Fern

time I left the church, Gretchen, a year into college, had sent shockwaves through Cornerstone's congregation with an unplanned pregnancy. She'd course-corrected with a "proper" marriage and more kids, so I expected to hear happy stories from Mickie about growing grandkids. "We haven't seen Gretchen in a long time," Mickie said, in a regretful tone but with confident eyes. "She isn't following the ways of the Lord."

Like me, Gretchen followed a different path. Perhaps she hoped her father's love would follow her or meet her somewhere in the middle. But the only spot for Gretchen was inside her father's identity, his church – if only she'd recognize her place. I went back in and sat in the chapel, which had remained unchanged for twenty years, thinking about this father and daughter and the tragedy of withholding love in this life for assurances in the next. Like James Baldwin, I knew the evangelical apparatus was not for me. It might have provided my father and many others with safety and assurances, but I had to walk away to find peace. In finding the wisdom of authors

CORNERSTONES

Elle Fern

like Baldwin, who urges one to look inward, to use the pain of history to cope with the present, I find the strength to write about my own views. And with each step in this journey to embrace my truth, I reclaim another piece of myself.

"Not everything that is faced can be changed, but nothing can be changed until it is faced."

– J. Baldwin

FATHER FIGURES

Clare Flanigan

In the church's suffocating basement, Father Mulvaney preaches about a woman's place. It's hot, and I shift back and forth on the hard, metal, folding chairs, then sit on my hands with my shoulders scrunched up to my ears, trying to make myself smaller. The fluorescent lights highlight every attribute that makes me different from the other adolescent girls, like the way my outfits aren't quite as put together. My knowledge of the bible is nothing compared to theirs.

Father Mulvaney peers down at the Bible-study class and says, "Women have a certain divine nature and traits to bring to a home that men just don't have. It's such a *special* gift."

If I retreat into the ruffles of my Sunday best, maybe I'll blend in. Maybe Father Mulvaney will look past me, because I don't want his dark, piercing eyes to break through my façade. I'm convinced he can see through me, leaving me vulnerable and exposed in this room full of perfect Christians.

FATHER FIGURES

Clare Flanigan

Before, when I had the courage to stray from the norm, I felt their wide-eyed stares, especially the day I asked, "Why can't women be priests?"

"Well," Father Mulvaney answered, "because that's the way God intended it. He didn't create women less than men, just differently."

For months, I'd tried to conform and keep up with the others, but my face eventually failed to conceal the truth. No matter how hard I prayed to believe Father Mulvaney's teachings, I couldn't. My own father's teachings wouldn't let me.

My dad was determined to stick to what he knew was right, even if it went against the Catholic beliefs he'd been raised with. Throughout my early childhood, he reminded me and my older sister, "Whatever your goals are, I'll stand behind you." I sometimes challenged the limits of his support with questions like, "What if I want to be the president? Or a lawyer, a movie star, or even a priest?" But his response remained the same: "I'll support you."

There are days when lingering Catholic guilt and fear still surge through my veins, especially when I

FATHER FIGURES

Clare Flanigan

spend time with religious friends, and a little devil appears on my shoulder. I don't see his horns poking out from under the halo, my head weighed down with thoughts of contrition, my cheeks flushed with shame. He's disguised himself as Jesus, whispering in my ear, "If you betray me, I will abandon you. Disown you. Leave you stranded in the fires of hell," and I feel myself shrink. But then I remember my father's colorful pillow dolls. I was six years old the day he introduced them to me.

I'd awakened from a nightmare, gasping for air. I'd been trapped on a cruise ship, and there was a chef with a handlebar mustache and curly lips chasing me. "I will cook you and serve you to the guests!" he shouted.

His large, puffy white hat made him even more menacing, as though something were hidden inside it. I ran to my parents on the ship, screaming for help, sobbing and begging, but they just laughed, engrossed in conversation. They ignored me and left me to fight the evil chef alone. I ran down the corridors of the ship, weaving in and out of its beige

Clare Flanigan

interior. And right when I'd finally lost him, I turned and saw the devilish man holding a long chopping knife. A flash of sunlight bounced off the sharp blade and onto my chest. For a few seconds I looked right into his sinister black eyes, then I awoke in a cold sweat, shaking, as if my body had fallen ten stories. The dream left a wound so deep and raw I couldn't find the words to describe it, and I felt ashamed. I didn't think anyone would understand my fear.

"How was your sleep, babydoll?" my mom asked the next morning. I wanted to tell her about the nightmare, but I felt a rock in my throat. I couldn't speak. I shrank, hung my head, and sat on my hands.

I walked to the school bus feeling vulnerable and violated, like the chef in the dream had actually attacked me. I headed to kindergarten and barely said a word. I couldn't concentrate, not on the games we played, or the pictures we colored. And the kids who squirted glue on their clothes during craft time weren't funny anymore. I dreaded going to sleep that night, and the whole way home on the bus, fear sat next to me like a bully.

FATHER FIGURES

Clare Flanigan

I finally made it inside and plopped down on our
flowery, red-and-yellow couch to watch TV with my
older sister Grace. I flashed her half-smiles every
time she looked to see my reaction to something
funny Hannah Montana had said.

By six o'clock, it was time to pick up my brother
and his friend from soccer. The idea of having to
perform another task with a painted-on smile filled
me with dread. In the car, unable to fight back tears,
I quietly sobbed into my gray, polyester seat so no
one would see.

We pulled into the driveway, and the impending
doom of the approaching night overwhelmed me. My
8:30 bedtime was quickly approaching. There didn't
seem to be a good time to get my mom alone, but I
couldn't keep my feelings bottled up anymore. I
decided I'd try to tell my dad. He was working at his
desk in the basement.

Walking down the basement stairs was almost as
scary as the anticipation of the nightmare repeating
itself. My anxiety grew with each step. What if he
didn't understand? I was worried he'd say something

Clare Flanigan

like, "Oh, Clare, that wasn't real. I'm busy," the same way he'd brushed me off in the dream. When I finally reached the doorway to his office, I saw that he was glued to the computer screen. My arms stiffened like sticks at my sides. I prayed the furrow in my brow would say everything he needed to know, but he didn't turn around to greet me.

I looked down at my feet and played with my fingernails, an unhealthy coping mechanism I've had since I was a baby, then finally mustered the courage to speak. "Um, Dad…"

He turned toward me in his swivel chair and let out a sigh, as if he'd had a long day. "Yeah, Clare B," he said; my nickname was "Clare B. Aebleskiver," which means Danish pancake. "What's going on?"

Avoiding eye contact, I managed to say, "Have you ever had a really scary dream and you can't stop thinking about it?" Tears rolled down my cheeks, then into my dad's button-down blue shirt. I felt relief; the fear lifted off my shoulders.

"I have something I want to show you," Dad said. He led me back up the stairs, through the kitchen, and

FATHER FIGURES

Clare Flanigan

down the hallway to my parents' room. I was confused when he opened the oak armoire. Rummaging around in a woven basket filled with various knick-knacks and trinkets, he pulled out a small wooden box.

"What's that?" I asked, my hopes deflating. *How would this little box solve any of my problems?*

"Open it up and see," Dad answered.

Unimpressed, I tugged open the top. Inside were four tiny dolls, each one dressed in elaborate clothes made of royal-blue, purple, and orange fabric. Their vibrant jewel tones mesmerized me, and I forgot my fear for a second. Their faces were too tiny to see their features. Everything about them was a mystery.

"You put them under your pillow," Dad explained, "and they protect you from all the bad dreams and demons." His explanation brought more comfort and security than he will ever know. He took me seriously, and that night I fell asleep with feelings of certainty and ease. I no longer had to carry the fear alone.

FATHER FIGURES

Clare Flanigan

I'm a junior in high school now, and every day, my dad reminds me of my intellect and abilities as a young woman. He would never ask me to shrink myself down. Instead, he picks me up from Feminist Club and wears a pin that says, "A Woman's Place is in The Resistance." When I watch him researching new interests, his love for learning inspires me to do the same. He challenges my mind and replenishes my library of books with the latest monthly read from his book club, Shakespeare, or a hometown author like Jeff Hobbs, who won the Los Angeles Times Book Prize for *The Short and Tragic Life of Robert Peace*. And on challenging days when I come home feeling beaten down, he pulls me in for a hug and says, "I'm so proud of how hard you work, Clare, and the person you've become."

Because of my dad's example, I've learned to never blindly follow any religion, organization, or person without fully understanding what they support. Unfortunately, organized religion and Catholicism introduced me to male leaders who made me feel small and worthless, men who'd rather

FATHER FIGURES

Clare Flanigan

silence my voice than hear my opinions. Religion has provided comfort and a sense of safety in my life, but it can be difficult to discern truth from fiction. Is it a tiny Jesus sitting on my shoulder or the devil in disguise? But all I need to do is remember the colorful dolls my dad gave me eleven years ago. Whenever I feel lonely or scared, I think back to those four little dolls. They still give me support and confidence, because they represent my father. And just like him, I believe they're here to protect me and guide me toward the truth.

MIS TRES HIJOS

Hannah Lee

SAMUEL

Pennsylvania, October 2013

My husband Pen and I sit in two orange, plastic chairs in a tiny hospital room that feels more like a broom closet. My hands are clasped and sweating. I wipe them off on my pant legs and then rest one hand on Pen's soft forearm. I try to breathe slowly and deeply, but it comes out in shaky spurts. Antiseptic fills my nostrils as I take another deep breath, and my heart speeds up as the door opens. Jen, our adoption counselor, pops her head in with a reassuring smile.

"Any minute now," she tells us. "How are you feeling?"

Instead of speaking, I make eye contact with her, nod, and take another slow, deep breath. She smiles again and closes the door. A few minutes later, there's another knock, and a nurse wheels Samuel into the room in a small, plexiglass cart.

I can barely breathe. *Is he really mine?*

MIS TRES HIJOS

Hannah Lee

He sleeps the deep sleep of a newborn, and I let myself take him in for the first time. He has thick, jet-black hair and enormous cheeks with a hint of a blush. His skin is smooth and perfect, the color of coffee just the way I like it. He is Mexican.

Gently, gingerly, I lift Samuel from the bassinet and kiss his soft round cheeks over and over. I cradle his warmth against my arms and chest. Then a strangeness moves through me – my body reminds me it cannot bear another loss. The previous year, my heart had been shattered when the baby girl we'd first adopted was removed from our home. Na'Jah – her birth mother had named her – lived with us four precious days. Depending on the state, birth mothers have a certain window of time to change their mind and choose to parent. We'd held Na'Jah, stayed up feeding her, rocking her, changing her, and loving her, and then her birth mother took her back.

If I lose Samuel, I won't know how *not* to love him. He is theoretically a stranger in my arms, but I am connected to him. The moment I learned his birth mother had chosen us, I fell to the kitchen floor.

MIS TRES HIJOS

Hannah Lee

"Yes! Yes!" I screamed, and reached for the back door, swinging it open and shrieking into the backyard, "Thank you, God! Thank you!" Containing the joy inside my kitchen seemed too small.

Although Na'Jah was the child I'd first given my heart to, it's Samuel who will transform me into a different person, a better version of myself, a mother to a beautiful brown boy, one of the great loves of my life.

***

Growing up, I felt adoption would be a part of my future. The idea of being a mother to a child who needed one seemed like the honor of a lifetime. As I reached adulthood, I was surprised to learn that not everyone shared this opinion. Pen and I made an agreement during our engagement to be child-free for the first five years of marriage. In year four, I shared my desire to begin our family through adoption. Pen didn't disagree, but he hadn't dreamed of adopting a child like I had; he needed more information. We attended an informational meeting

Hannah Lee

at a local adoption agency and heard perspectives from birth parents, adoptees, and adoptive parents. For me, the meeting confirmed this was the right path, and it persuaded Pen as well.

Eventually, we learned that over 50% of the birth mothers who used our adoption agency were Black, but the majority of adoptive families sought white babies. Since we knew our family would love and support a child of any race, we asked that our profile be shown to birth families of color. We didn't need a baby to look like us to belong to our hearts. We attended more informational trainings, specifically geared toward transracial adoptions, and understood that we'd likely be placed with a Black child. However, Samuel was the only Hispanic adoption our agency arranged that year.

Fate had aligned the stars to bring us our little Mexicano. He made sense with us. I spoke Spanish and soon plugged myself into Hispanic communities. I volunteered at night and taught English as a Second Language to adult immigrants. I loved my students, their hearts, their work ethic, their humor, their

Hannah Lee

heartbreaking stories, their resilience, and their relentless hope. Students soon became friends who invited me into their homes and taught me to make tortillas, quesadillas, and tamales from scratch. We watched our children play together at the park and met for ice cream in town. Our adoption trainings had taught us the importance of plugging into communities that represented our child's heritage. Everything felt right as we immersed ourselves in Samuel's culture.

After Samuel arrived, no second child came to us biologically. Pen and I briefly discussed the option of fertility treatments, but decided not to pursue it. We wanted to be a family to a child who needed one, not because we needed a child to share our genetic makeup. It took intentionality to connect with the Hispanic community, but we'd made significant progress. Dividing our energies towards a third culture seemed unfair to Samuel, and we wanted him to feel a cultural connection with a future sibling. We'd read and heard numerous accounts of adoptees experiencing the difficulty of being the only person of color in their family. I hoped that Samuel and his future sibling would look at one another and feel comforted that they weren't alone, and know we valued their rich heritage. Still, Hispanic adoptions were rare within our agency. So, we waited, and waited. And then came Marco.

***

MARCO

Delaware, September 2017

"Marin's saying her final goodbyes now. Marco will arrive in just a moment," our adoption worker says. I feel my heart clench and my eyes follow suit. My greatest joy is another woman's greatest loss.

At Marin's request, we waited a day to meet him. Then, at the very moment she placed him in my arms, he let out a joyous shout, as if to say, "Yeah! You're here!" I wanted to smother his face with kisses but, once again, found myself holding back. *What if Marin changes her mind? Should I let myself love*

MIS TRES HIJOS

Hannah Lee

him? How is it possible I already do? I looked over at Marin, sitting on the hospital bed, and saw her smile at me with tears in her eyes. I still can't imagine how painful, yet joyful, it was for her to see me fall in love with her son. I reflected on what our previous adoption counselor had shared with me: "the space where a birthmother meets the woman who will mother her child is considered 'holy ground.'"

Marco's wrapped in a soft, white blanket, wearing a matching white cap with a blue pompom. I gaze down at him and read the blue lettering on his cap. It says, "Delivered with love." *So very much,* I think. Soon after, Pen and I drive home with our precious son, Samuel's little brother.

I try not to hold back this time. I cover his tiny face with kisses and soak in the heat of his little body. I breathe in his soft, sweet, warmth -- a smell so familiar, like coming home, but also new to me. Marco looks nothing like Samuel did as a baby; his complexion is fair. His cheeks aren't as round. As I hold his body close to mine, I notice his light-olive complexion. It brings out my skin's pink undertones.

101

MIS TRES HIJOS

Hannah Lee

He is longer and slimmer than Samuel was. He is different, and he is perfect.

We click his infant carrier into his car seat, and I reach for my phone to let my mother know when to expect us. I notice the date: September 19, 2017. It's exactly four years to the day that Na'Jah left our arms. Four years earlier, Pen and I had sobbed in each other's arms. Afterward, I lay on the living-room floor in a heap, my vision blurred by loss, staring at the clock as the minutes went by. And now I'm here beside Marco, stroking his soft face, ecstatic to introduce him to Samuel. I know, though, that another mother is lying on the floor now, her vision blurred by tears.

Marin looks like me. She's petite and thin, with fair skin and eyes and curly blonde hair. Marco's birth father is Mexican, and his complexion resembles Samuel's. Samuel knew we were adopting another child, and each night when we prayed together as a family, he repeated, "Dear Gahd, peas bwing a baby to da house."

MIS TRES HIJOS

Hannah Lee

The night we brought Marco home, Samuel stood proudly over his brother's bassinet and said, "Dear Gahd, tank you fah mah baby." He couldn't stop gazing at "his" baby and kept trying to climb into the bassinet to be closer to him.

Although Marco is half-Mexican, his light-skinned genes prevailed, and I find myself thinking, *he'll be able to pass for a white kid.* The thought sickens me, and I feel embarrassed, but also thankful that Marco won't have to experience the racism woven into the fabric of my country. But I'm sickened that Samuel will. I'm also thankful that people don't immediately know Marco is adopted when he's out with Pen or me in public. And I'm heartbroken that compared to Marco, Samuel will be labeled "the adopted one."

***

MIS TRES HIJOS

Hannah Lee

PABLO

New Jersey, March 2020

"Mommy, I gotta go potty. NOW!" Samuel shouts.

"I understand, buddy, just give us a minute," I tell him. "Remember, this isn't our house."

It's the beginning of the pandemic and the first day of the shutdown. Schools are closed, so both Samuel and Marco are with Pen and me. We all stand on the front stoop of Josh and Karen's home. They're the New Jersey couple who've cared for Pablo for the past four days; adoption agencies often choose to place babies in interim care while a birth family finalizes their adoption plan. Karen has spent the first sleepless nights with Pablo, and I hate that I've lost this time with him. I knock lightly on the storm door. COVID lockdown has just begun, and before the door opens, I wonder if it's okay for Pen and me to shake Josh and Karen's hands. *Will we bring sickness to our family?*

MIS TRES HIJOS

Hannah Lee

"Hello! Welcome! Come on in!" Josh says, smiling and holding the door open like we've know each other for years. Worrying about a handshake now seems silly, especially since Pablo has been in Josh and Karen's care for several days and breathing the same air.

Samuel rushes inside, followed by Marco. Karen holds Pablo, and I try to peek at his face. She quickly walks over and places him right in my arms. His dark little face and hands are visible beneath his onesie. He's wrapped in a white blanket with the words "I love you" printed all over it. Karen has loved him, but I also wish his first days of life had been with me. I take in the wonder of him: he is Guatemalan, and his skin is darker than his birth mother's.

"I have to go right now!" yells Samuel. My head jerks up, and I hear Josh say, "Bathroom? Right over here." He opens a nearby door and switches the light on. Marco runs past Samuel and shuts the door.

"Hey!" Samuel yells.

"It was actually Sam that needed the bathroom," Pen explains to Josh.

MIS TRES HIJOS

Hannah Lee

"No problem, we have another bathroom upstairs."

Samuel bounds up the stairs and makes himself at home, which gives Pen a chance to stand beside me and admire Pablo. He places his strong hand on Pablo's tiny body, then strokes his son's dark cheeks. I can't stop staring, taking in our new son. He's a little tank, and the largest of the boys as a baby.

Karen and Josh move us into their family room, and we sit on the couch. Pablo is still in my arms, and Samuel and Marco clamber around us, trying to see their baby brother. They climb and perch and lay kisses all over Pablo's face. He barely stirs.

Looking at these three beautiful boys, I'm overcome with joy. I love them with gratitude and with abandon. I no longer hold back. I know I am their mother, and they are my sons: *mis tres hijos*.

NOT ALL FAMILIES

Hannah Lee

October 2021

Brandywine Valley, Pennsylvania

After eight years of motherhood, I'd grown into a confident parent, but my stomach tensed the morning I pulled into Highland Orchards. It's just north of Kennett Square, in the Brandywine Valley of Pennsylvania, where we live. Pablo and I were on one of our first outings together since the pandemic began. With three little ones at home, I was extra cautious. I wore a mask, even though we'd mostly be outside.

The sun was bright in the blue Autumn sky, the air warm but tempered with a cool breeze. Pablo was a toddler, and at nineteen months, able to walk the grounds with me. He tottered along on the uneven ground, his chubby hand holding my fingers to steady himself. We visited the little goat pen, and I watched his face break into a smile. He shrieked with

Hannah Lee

delight, picking up sweet-smelling hay and feeding it to the goats from the palm of his tiny hand.

After bidding the goats goodbye, we headed to the open-air market, and I grabbed a mini shopping cart. There were bins full of juicy Honeycrisp apples, and their fresh scent engulfed us as I started to fill the cart with baby pumpkins and bumpy gourds. Pablo pointed and beckoned and asked to hold each little pumpkin before it went in the cart.

We were near the swinging door to the bakery, and the fragrance of warm apple cider donuts wafted in our direction. We followed the cinnamon-sugar scent inside, and I put Pablo in the shopping cart and ordered a dozen donuts to take home. As we waited for the latest batch, several customers said hello to Pablo. Behind their masks, I could tell they were smiling at him. I smiled back with my eyes.

The man behind the counter handed me the white bag of fresh donuts. The bottom was moist with buttery goodness; I'd never make it home without sampling one. I reached into my purse for my wallet,

Hannah Lee

but Pablo's dimpled hand was wrapped around my index finger.

"Love, Mama needs her hand back. I can't grab my wallet," I said.

"Mama. Ma-Ma! Mom-eee!" he sang, smiling and kicking his feet. His dark eyes sparkled, and I felt my heart flutter. I stroked the smooth skin of his cheeks, which were the color of brown sugar; listened to him laugh; and felt amazed to be here again. I'd first experienced this surreal magic when Samuel was born but didn't believe it was possible to feel it twice, let alone three times.

"Dame un besito," I said. *Give me a smooch.* I leaned down and planted exaggerated kisses all over his cheeks. He laughed and let go of my finger. I dug my wallet out of my purse.

"Will that be all?" the middle-aged woman working the register asked.

"Yes," I said, feeling anxious because she wasn't wearing a mask. I wanted to protect Pablo, and hoped I hadn't made a mistake taking him to a public place.

109

NOT ALL FAMILIES

Hannah Lee

"Is he yours?" she asked. She smiled, and my body relaxed.

She means no harm, I thought. It was a familiar question; the people who asked generally didn't have malicious intent. My husband, Pen, and I have light complexions, hair, and eyes, which doesn't match the complexion, hair, and eyes of our sons. Maybe she wanted me to verify that I was Pablo's mother before saying, "Your son is beautiful!" Her smile made me hopeful that she, too, was enamored with my little boy. Since he was too young to be vaccinated, I'd rarely experienced strangers doting on him. The pandemic had robbed us of that.

I heard myself say, "Yes."

"You'd never know it," the woman replied.

Startled, I look at her face again and saw her tight grin. My heart sank. Her eyes no longer met mine. Instead, she busily punched buttons on the register. Hot blood rushed from my chest to my neck, then into my face. *Don't react,* I told myself, even though I knew I was turning red. I swallowed hard and

Hannah Lee

focused my eyes on her hands ringing up the pumpkins, gourds, and donuts.

"Yes," I said again with pride. "He's *all* mine."

Handing me the receipt, she leaned over Pablo with a smirk and blurted out, "Was Mommy even there?"

My mouth fell open inside my mask. It was as though she'd hit me squarely in the chest and knocked the air out of my lungs. I couldn't formulate words. She looked back up at me, seemingly pleased with herself, and I quickly backed away, holding Pablo close.

As I walked to the car, I chastised myself for not confronting the woman. *You taught middle school Spanish for fifteen years, Hannah! Why weren't you more prepared?* As a teacher, I was proud of my quick responses to ignorant and racist comments by adolescent students. But this was a grown woman, and her cruelty rendered me speechless.

On the drive home, I wondered if she would have done this had Pablo been older. And what would I have said if he could understand?

NOT ALL FAMILIES

Hannah Lee

I'd spent so much time in isolation during the pandemic, I'd forgotten that comments like these were woven into the story of our family. Pen is fair, tall, broad-shouldered, and redheaded. I have blue eyes and blonde hair. Without copious amounts of sunblock, we look like boiled lobsters in the summer. Our family's physical differences have produced many comments and questions from complete strangers who feel they're entitled to intimate details of our children's birth families. On one occasion, before Pablo was born and we were still a family of four with Samuel and our other son Marco, a white parent we didn't know approached Pen during a birthday party.

"Are they yours?"

"Yes. Those two are mine," Pen answered, as the boys devoured pizza.

"Are they brothers?"

"Yes," he said. "They're my sons."

Not catching the cue, the woman pressed on.

"Right, but are they *really* brothers?"

NOT ALL FAMILIES

Hannah Lee

"Yes, they are *really* brothers," Pen replied, more calmly than I would have.

Samuel, our oldest, has brown skin, dark brown eyes, and jet-black hair. Marco has much lighter skin and hair. If Pen and I were out with Marco, without Samuel and Pablo, we didn't receive the second glances we're accustomed to now. While I understood this parent's curiosity, she could have asked, "Are they biological brothers?" But why did she feel privy to that information? Why do white people, in general, feel they have the right to ask?

Currently, the boys only know pieces of their adoption stories because of their age and comprehension level. They are still too young to understand the inappropriateness and ignorance of comments from strangers. But because my children's skin color differs from mine, and from each other, we'll continue to face questions. And as they grow older and spend time with more people who do not look like them, the window of "what they don't know won't hurt them" is rapidly closing.

NOT ALL FAMILIES

Hannah Lee

Since becoming a mother, I've realized just how privileged I am as a white woman. Never did I consider the dangers my future children would face wearing a sweatshirt with a hood, nor could I imagine how they'd fear for their safety as teenagers, should they be stopped by the police. But these scenarios are commonplace in the daily lives of Black and brown families.

Samuel is nine now, and reading at a 3rd-grade level. The *Harry Potter* books are among his favorites, and I've come to cherish our nightly reading routine, even though some nights I'm exhausted and need my own bed. But I know these bedtime stories together are fleeting. We open the book and learn that Harry has once again been treated badly by his cousin Dudley. When the chapter ends, we close the book for the night and prepare for "snuggle time," which transforms into, "Please lie beside me, Mom, but don't breathe on me or near me. And don't touch me either – it's too hot." He takes a moment to settle into a suitable spot, then says,

NOT ALL FAMILIES

Hannah Lee

"Mom…today we learned about segregation in school."

I turn to face him, my heartbeat speeding up, but I attempt a calm reply. "Oh, really? That's good. It's important to learn about segregation. What do you think it means?"

His large, dark eyes stare deeply into mine. "It means that people with dark skin weren't allowed to be around white people." He continues to stare at me as if willing me to say his teacher was mistaken. I fight a wave of nausea picturing him next to some of his white classmates, learning about racism.

Several months ago, I tried to initiate the subject by reading him a book about Jackie Robinson, and *Antiracist Baby* by Ibram X. Kendi. I started the conversation, but Samuel quickly ended it, informing me he was finished with story time and wanted to play video games.

But now that I have his attention, I say, "Yes, baby… it's a horrible part of our country's history. I'm so thankful that people fought hard to make

Hannah Lee

change, because our skin color has nothing to do with our value as a person."

"But, Mommy," he says, "it means we couldn't have been together."

I hate this moment. I hate that people with skin like mine hold this history, and I hate that it's still a part of our present. I haven't been honest with Samuel, and I doubt his teachers have either. So far, I've approached the subject like a history lesson: *Segregation used to be a thing. People fought to make change. Martin Luther King used nonviolence to fight for equality.* And although Dr. King's dream of children of different skin colors holding hands has come true, I haven't told Samuel the whole truth. I haven't told him that racism and hatred are still alive and well in our country. I haven't told him that there are people who will judge him by the color of his skin and not the content of his character. I hate that I can't take this burden from him, that I can't even help him carry it; my privilege is impenetrable.

Nonetheless, I know I must prepare myself for the difficult conversations that lie ahead, both with

Hannah Lee

my boys and with strangers who question our family. So I will try my best to remain calm the way Pen does when someone looks at us and says, "But is he *really* yours?" Because, just as our sage adoption instructor suggested in one of our training sessions, I can lead with, "Not all families look alike." And on days when a white person thinks it's appropriate to ask where my Hispanic sons are from, my response will be, "They're from *America*. How about your kids?"

Made in the USA
Middletown, DE
14 July 2023

35185865R00066